LISA YUNKER WELZ

BOOK SERIES BY FIG FACTOR MEDIA

WordPower Book Series

© Copyright 2021, Fig Factor Media, LLC.
All rights reserved.

All rights reserved. No portion of this book may be reproduced by mechanical, photographic or electronic process, nor may it be stored in a retrieval system, transmitted in any form or otherwise be copied for public use or private use without written permission of the copyright owner.

It is sold with the understanding that the publisher and the individual authors are not engaged in the rendering of psychological, legal, accounting or other professional advice. The content and views in each chapter are the sole expression and opinion of its author and not necessarily the views of Fig Factor Media, LLC.

For more information, contact:

Fig Factor Media, LLC | www.figfactormedia.com

Cover Design & Layout by Juan Pablo Ruiz
Printed in the United States of America

ISBN: 978-1-957058-03-0
Library of Congress Control Number: 2021923562

DEDICATION

I would like to dedicate this book to my wonderful husband, Mike, our awesome kids, Eric, Tim, and Katie, and their special people, Kylie Knur, Lindsey Smith, and Sean Nadeau—each of you make my heart happy.

To my sister, Teresa Hartford, and the Yunker and Welz families—I've been blessed to have amazing family members that I love to spend time with. In my heart there are no in-laws, only family.

To a few special girlfriends who are like sisters to me—I love you!

Finally, a special dedication to my mom, aka Granny, Marie Yunker, for being my ever-present example and inspiration. I want to be you when I grow up, and always have.

ACKNOWLEDGMENTS

I would like to thank Jackie Camacho-Ruiz for extending this honor of authorship to me and her belief that I would have something worthwhile to contribute. Kylie Knur and Gaby Hernandez-Franch for their encouragement and support during this process. Anna Fisher for her insightful suggestions and edits. The Fig Factor Media team who turned my efforts into a beautiful book. I offer my thanks and appreciation for the time and talent each of you have spent on my behalf. You are, indeed, the best.

INTRO

From the time I was a little girl, life revolved around my family. Many weekends were spent with my grandparents on the farm in Mokena, Illinois. I listened to the pigs make noise all night, fed the cows their vitamins, played frisbee with my sister and cousins in the pasture, and nearly drowned in soybeans in the grainery one Sunday afternoon.

I also helped my grandma peel bushels of apples, bake cakes, pies, and apple bread. She taught me how to set a table, iron tablecloths, work in the garden, mash potatoes, and encouraged me to learn how to make a grasshopper ice cream drink with my Uncle Ron.

Summers were spent together in Wyoming and Montana, camping, hiking, swimming, and fishing. I put thousands of miles on my bike, worked to achieve an epic tan, and enjoyed a carefree life that I didn't appreciate as much then as I do now.

No matter where we were, my parents took the time to teach me thousands of little lessons—and some big ones--about honesty, integrity, responsibility, kindness, and thinking about what I said before I said it.

My husband, Mike, and I took our experiences and, in our own way, gave similar ones to our children, Eric, Tim, and Katie. We added time at Pelican Lake, Wisconsin, where we vacation and snowmobile as often as possible.

It is my hope that this little book encourages you to sit down and think about the memories you have made with your own family—and plans for the ones you have yet to make.

Throughout my life, nothing has been more important than family. Family is at the core of everything I do and receives consideration in every important decision I make.

WHAT IS YOUR TOP PRIORITY?

As I grew up, I realized that families come in all shapes and sizes. While some are close-knit, like my own, others are full of hurt that drives them apart. I learned not to assume that all families are like mine, to be careful not to hurt others, and to do everything in my power to keep our family close.

WHEN DID YOU REALIZE THAT ALL FAMILIES ARE NOT THE SAME?

My dad died from glioblastoma brain cancer at 53 years old. I will do anything to spend time with my family because I understand how short time can be. We enjoy hanging out and talking, working on projects together, cooking, shopping, and playing games.

WHAT DO YOU ENJOY DOING WITH YOUR FAMILY?

Family also includes those who you choose. Those who don't share your blood but share your heart.

For me, that also includes those special people my adult kids have chosen whether they are dating, engaged, or married.

HOW DO YOU WELCOME PEOPLE INTO YOUR FAMILY?

My grandmother, Laverne Yunker, taught me that family could include a difficult, sad old woman named Mildred, who disliked green beans and never smiled, even on holidays. Through my grandmother's actions, I learned to be kind and generous to everyone and respect our differences.

MY GRANDPARENTS HAD A HUGE INFLUENCE ON MY LIFE. WHO HAS INFLUENCED YOUR LIFE?

I learned from my parents that family is about love and support. In my own family, when we are together, we talk about the big and the small; we tease, laugh, give advice, love, and support each other. No matter what is happening, if one of us needs love and support, everyone is there to help them.

HOW DO YOU SHOW LOVE IN YOUR FAMILY?

Sometimes our family might yell and argue, but we always do our best not to go to bed angry. This is very important to me, even if that means apologizing before
I'm ready.

HOW DOES YOUR FAMILY DEAL WITH ARGUMENTS?

Silly moments create lifelong memories. At dinner one Sunday, my dad asked for the pickles. My uncle pretended to be a quarterback and threw a pickle like a football from one end of the table to the other. We weren't sure that grandma approved, but we all laughed and spun another thread to tie us closer together. Every time I think back to that day, it brings a spark of joy to my heart.

STORIES ABOUT FAMILY MEMBERS ARE MY FAVORITE BECAUSE THEY MAKE ME FEEL CLOSE TO THEM, WHETHER THEY LIVE FAR AWAY OR ARE NO LONGER WITH US. WHAT ARE YOUR FAVORITE FAMILY STORIES?

If I could do one thing over, I would tell my children stories about my dad—their grandfather—when they were little. The pain from losing him kept me from talking about him until they were teenagers. They would have loved him as much as I did.

HOW DO YOU KEEP YOUR FAMILY MEMORIES ALIVE?

My mom inspires me every day. She lived with us for three months after our twins were born, has been there for me through two major surgeries, puppy sat every weekday for months so I could work, and has shown her love for our family in a million more ways.

DO YOU HAVE A FAMILY MEMBER WHO INSPIRES YOU?

My husband's family has a knack for remembering every silly or stupid thing that has ever happened in their lives and then teasing each other about it, over and over throughout the years.

WHAT ARE SOME THINGS YOUR FAMILY LIKES TO TEASE YOU ABOUT?

My grandparents lived on a dairy farm and always invited anyone who stopped by to join them for a meal. Any visitor was treated as part of the family—especially on holidays. We love this tradition, and we enjoy inviting others to join us whenever possible.

WHAT ARE YOUR FAMILY TRADITIONS?

ABOUT AUTHOR

Lisa Welz is a freelance copywriter who loves her family and her grandpets, Montana, Nash, Frankie, and Doug. She is part of the JJR Marketing team, helps authors at Fig Factor Media, was a local journalist for 13 years, and before that, a stay-at-home mom, office manager for a commercial roofing company, and a bartender--which has come in handy during the pandemic. She has been married to the love of her life, Mike, for 31 years, and has three adult children who she adores--Eric, Tim, and Katie. Lisa would rather read books than watch TV, loves music, is addicted to coffee, loves to travel, and enjoys spending time with her girlfriends.

www.ingramcontent.com/pod-product-compliance
Lightning Source LLC
Chambersburg PA
CBHW041235240426
43673CB00011B/341

The Illustrator

I'm only a computer
I'm really not too smart
A human takes the "Ficial"
And turns it into "Art!"

A Note from the Author

Last year, I wrote *Dinosaur Symphony,* which is really a book to go along with a piece of music I am doing that teaches kids about the classical symphony orchestra by comparing each instrument to a different dinosaur. It was a one-off. But, for some reason ... it was more popular than my "real" books! *Dinosaur Ballet* was a hit too, so I suppose *Dinosaur Opera* was inevitable; I am, after all, an opera composer, and artistic director of an opera company.

But it caused more agony than the others, because opera plots can be pretty gruesome. And yet, they are really no gorier than the *real* Grimm's fairy tales. Cinderella's sisters having their eyes pecked out by crows, Sleeping Beauty assaulted in her sleep, Little Red Riding Hood being cut out of the wolf's tummy, and other horrors are as scary as anything in an opera. But, unlike with fairy tales, there are few "disneyfied" versions of opera plots. So, please, I urge caution, and have noted the "recommended age" for this book as somewhat higher than the others in the series.

Even so, every kid is different ... as is every grownup.

When the time came to illustrate the book, I turned to Artificial "Intelligence" for help, which was a little frustrating. It seems that AI knows less that most four-year-olds about what some dinosaurs looked like. It certainly has little clue about opera. A lot of tweaking and prodding, and the results are pretty entertaining. But please give the silicon guy a break. "Artificial" for sure; the jury is still out on "intelligence."

Honestly, this book shouldn't even exist. Is it even really a children's book? But I do know kids who go to the opera regularly,

Let's just say that it's not *just* a "children's book" but one that can be enjoyed by children of *all* ages. From kids with adult aspirations to adults in their second childhood, I hope this little foible of mine will be enjoyed by my fellow nerds throughout the world.

—S.P. Somtow

www.ingramcontent.com/pod-product-compliance
Lightning Source LLC
Chambersburg PA
CBRC090910230426
43673CB00017B/422